Let's Talk About

FIGHTING

Let's Talk About
FIGHTING

By JOY WILT BERRY

Illustrated by John Costanza
Edited by Orly Kelly
Designed by Jill Losson

GROLIER ENTERPRISES CORP.

Let's talk about FIGHTING.

FIGHTING can be harmful. When people fight, they often hurt each other's bodies and feelings. They may also damage or destroy each other's things.

Thus, fighting is not good.

When you are angry you must *never do anything to hurt yourself or another person.* Do not hit, kick, bite, scratch, pinch, or pull someone's hair.

You must *never damage or destroy things* when you are angry. Do not hit, kick, or throw things that can be damaged or destroyed.

If you do not want to fight, stay away from people who always make you angry.

Do not play too roughly if you do not want to fight. Someone usually gets hurt when people play roughly. Often the person who has been hurt gets angry and wants to fight.

If you do not want to fight, do not spend too much time with one person. When people get tired of being around each other, they often fight.

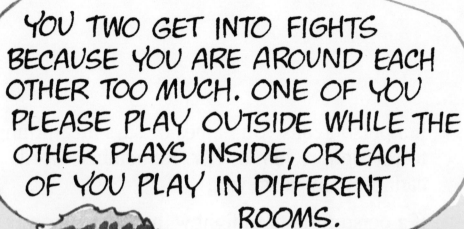

If a person calls you names or says mean things to you, ignore him or her. Remember, words cannot really harm you.

If a person wants to fight with you, walk away from him or her. If the person follows you, ask an adult to help you.

You can solve the problems you have with other people without fighting.

When someone does something to make you angry, do not do anything right away. If you act too quickly, you may get into a fight.

Slowly count to ten when you are angry. This will give you some time to *calm down.*

After you have calmed down, *talk with the other person*. Do not scream or call names. Do not say bad things.

Talk about yourself and how you feel. Tell the other person why you are angry and what you think should be done.

Give the other person a chance to talk. *Listen* carefully. Be respectful of his or her thoughts and feelings. Try to understand the other side of the story.

After you and other person have said
everything that needs to be said, decide what
to do. There are several ways to solve a problem:

- You can do what the other person wants
  to do.
- The other person can do what you
  want to do.
- You both can give in a little without
  giving in completely. This is called
  compromising.

If the other person and you cannot decide what to do, ask someone to help you. Be sure to go to a person who is old enough and wise enough to be fair.

When you ask someone to help you, do not try to get that person to agree with you. Do not try to make him or her angry at the other person.

It is best for everyone when you solve your problems without fighting.

When you fight, you may hurt yourself or another person. You may also damage or destroy something.

This is why you should not fight.